Amelia Boman

COPYRIGHT NOTICE
All rights reserved. No part of this publication may be reproduced, distributed, or transmitted in any form or by any means, including photocopying, recording, or other electronic or mechanical methods, without the prior written permission of the author, except in the case of brief quotations embodied in critical reviews.

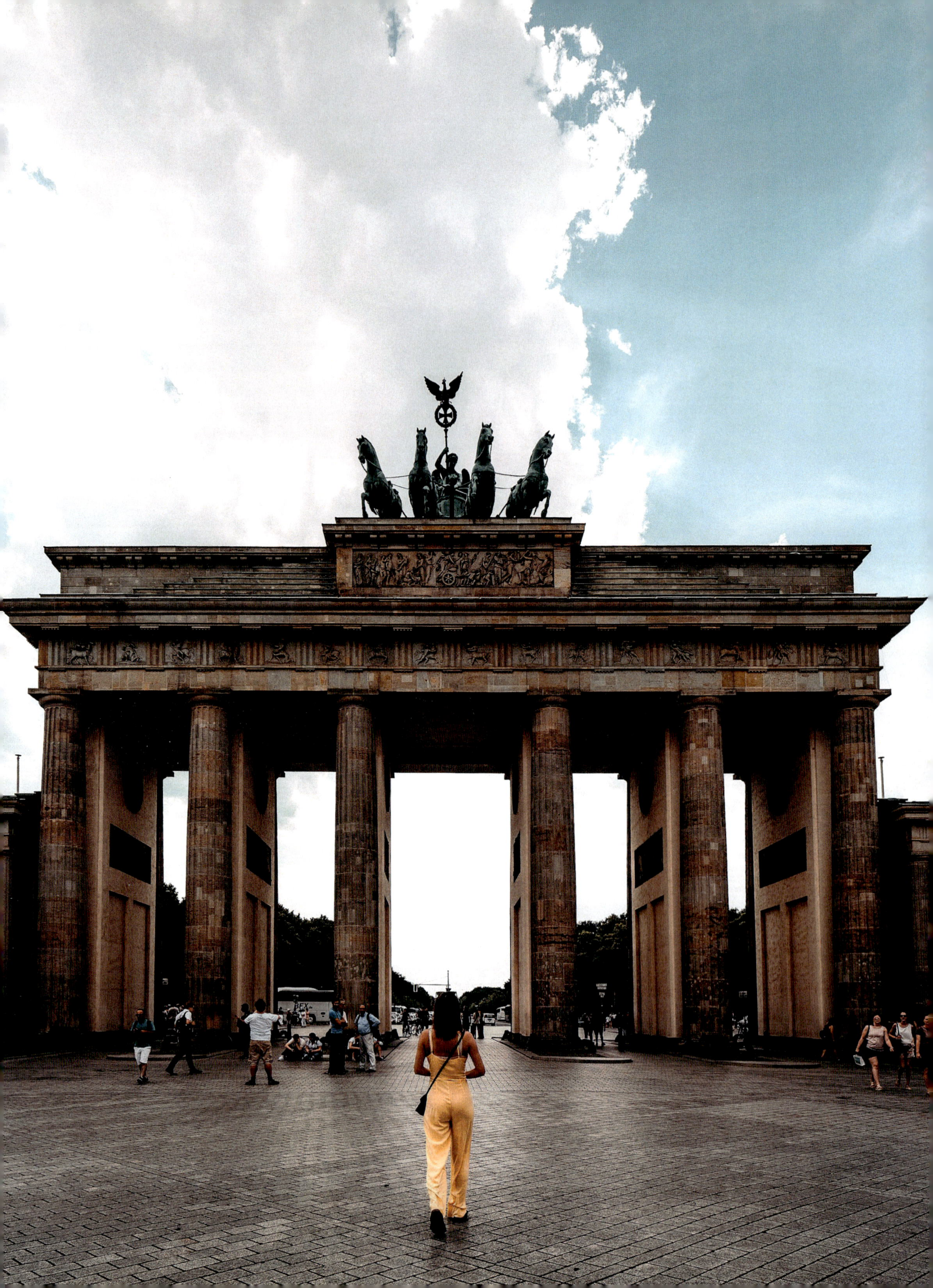

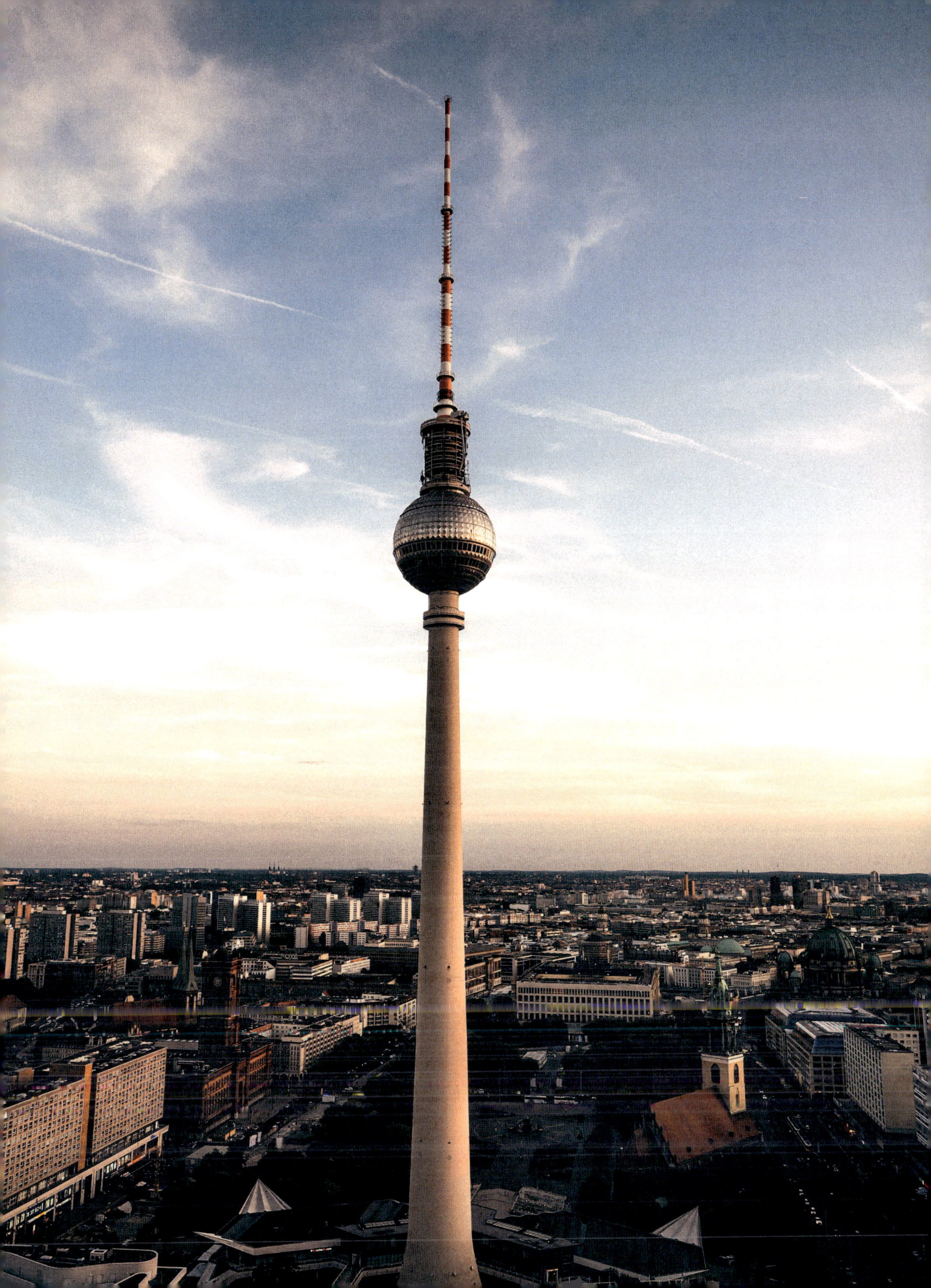

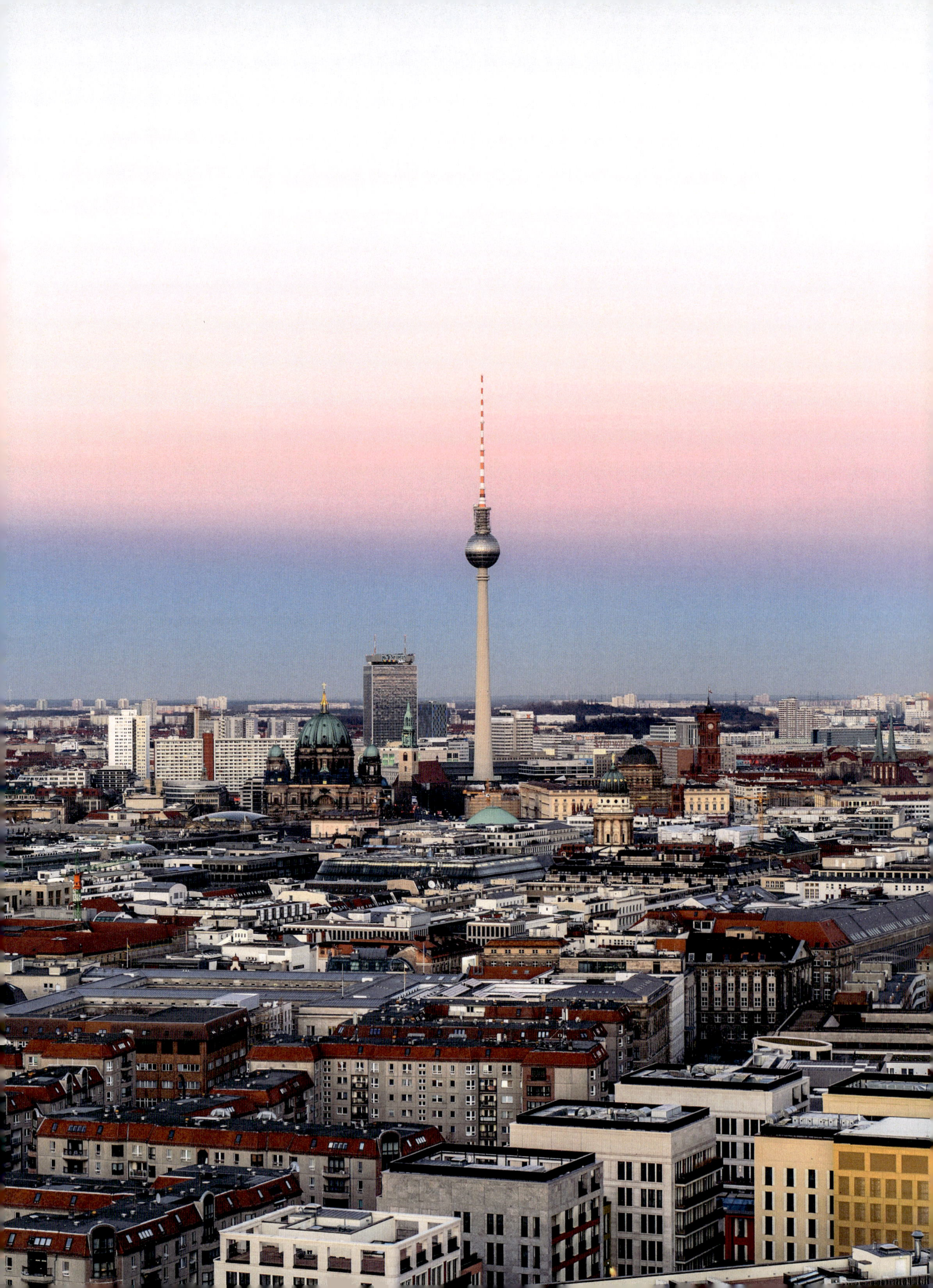

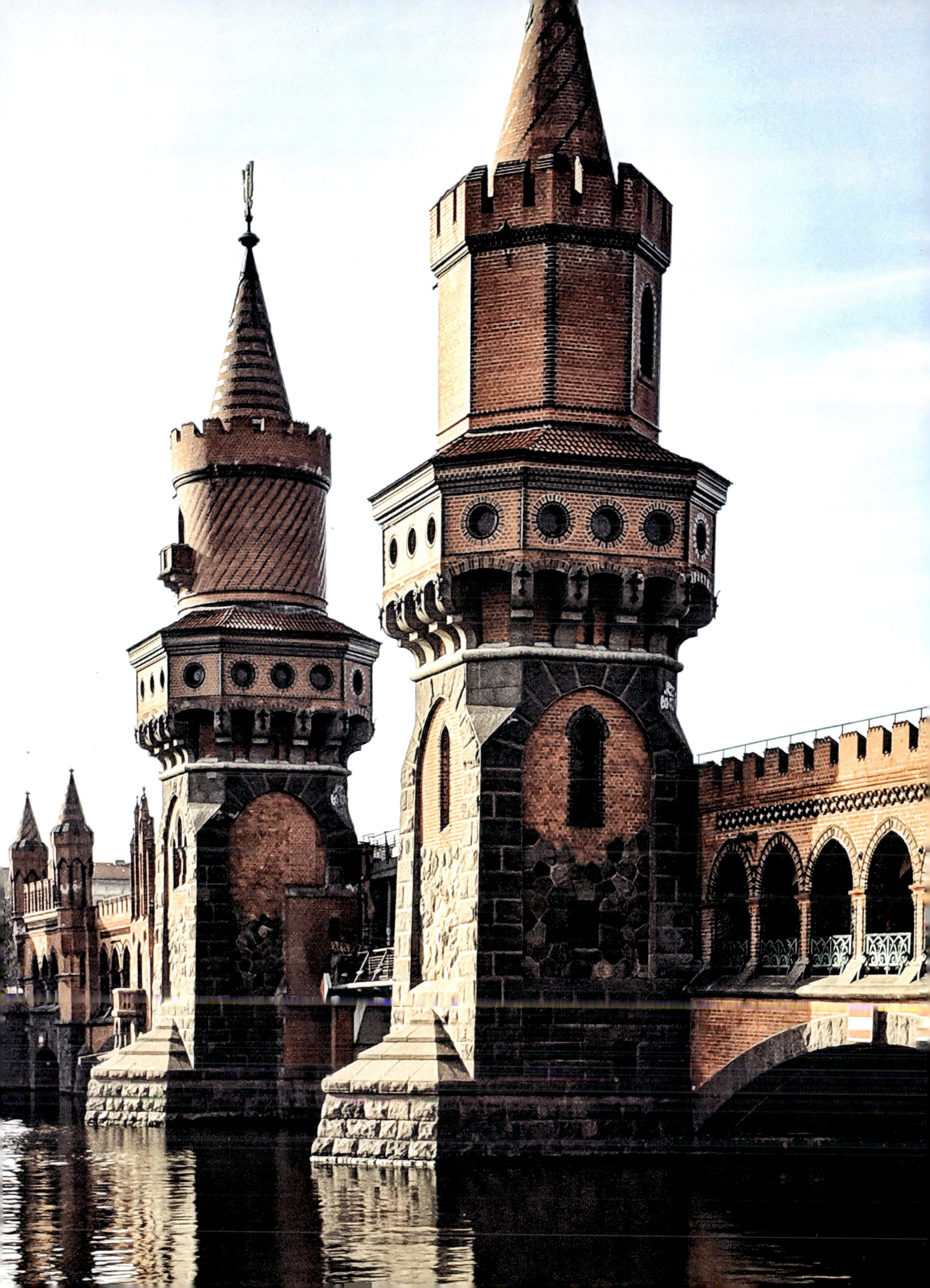

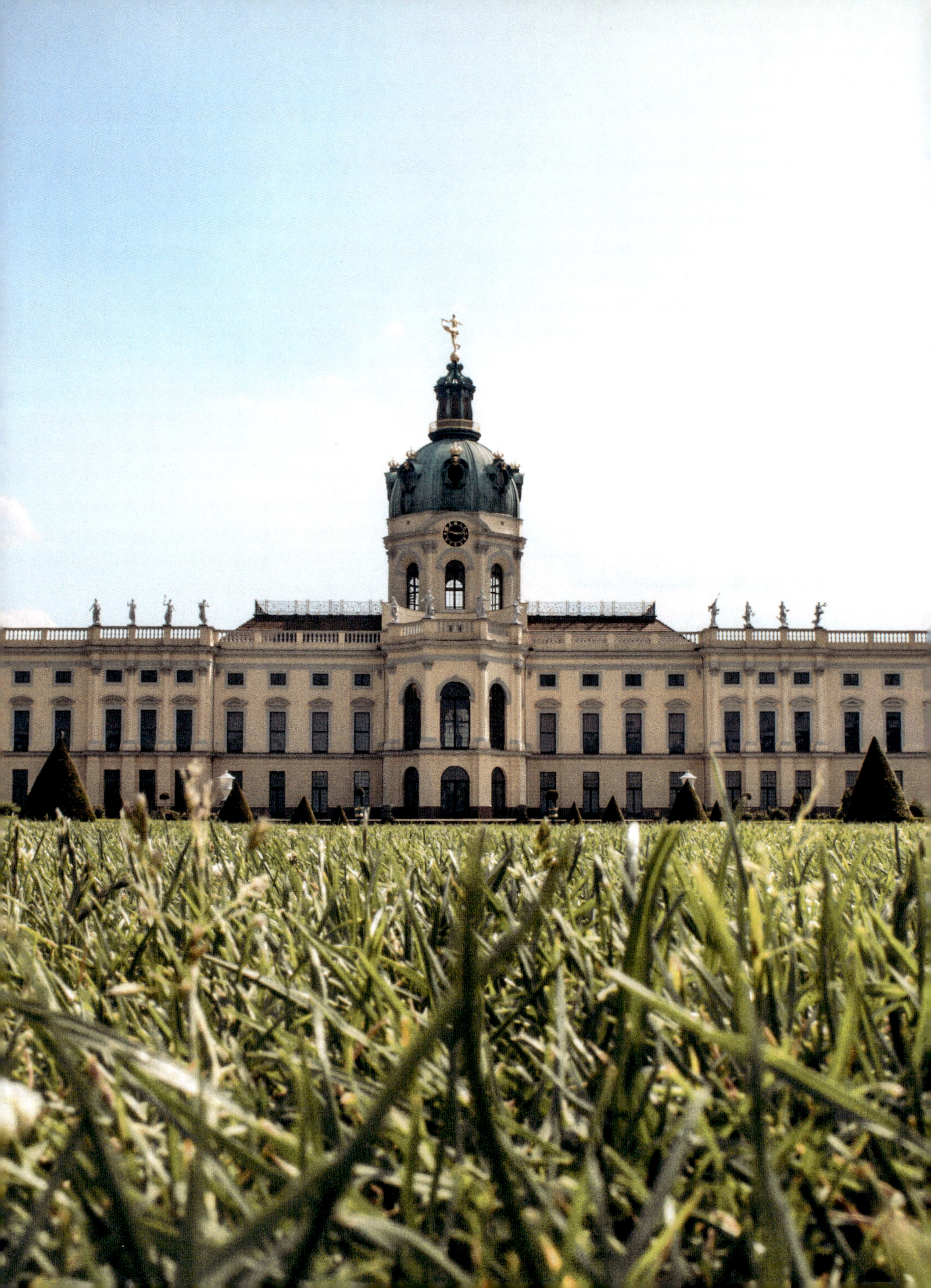

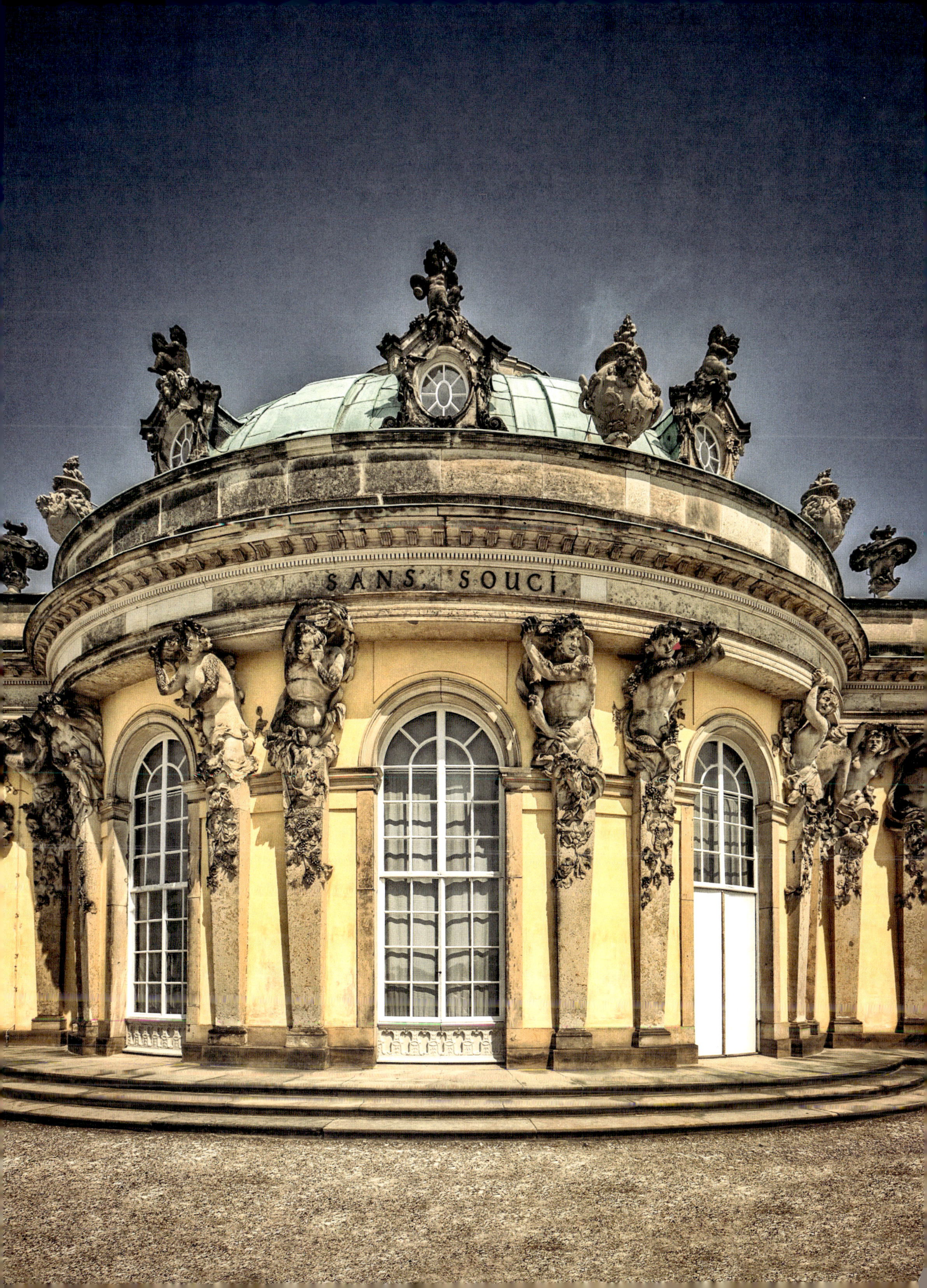
SANS, SOUCI.

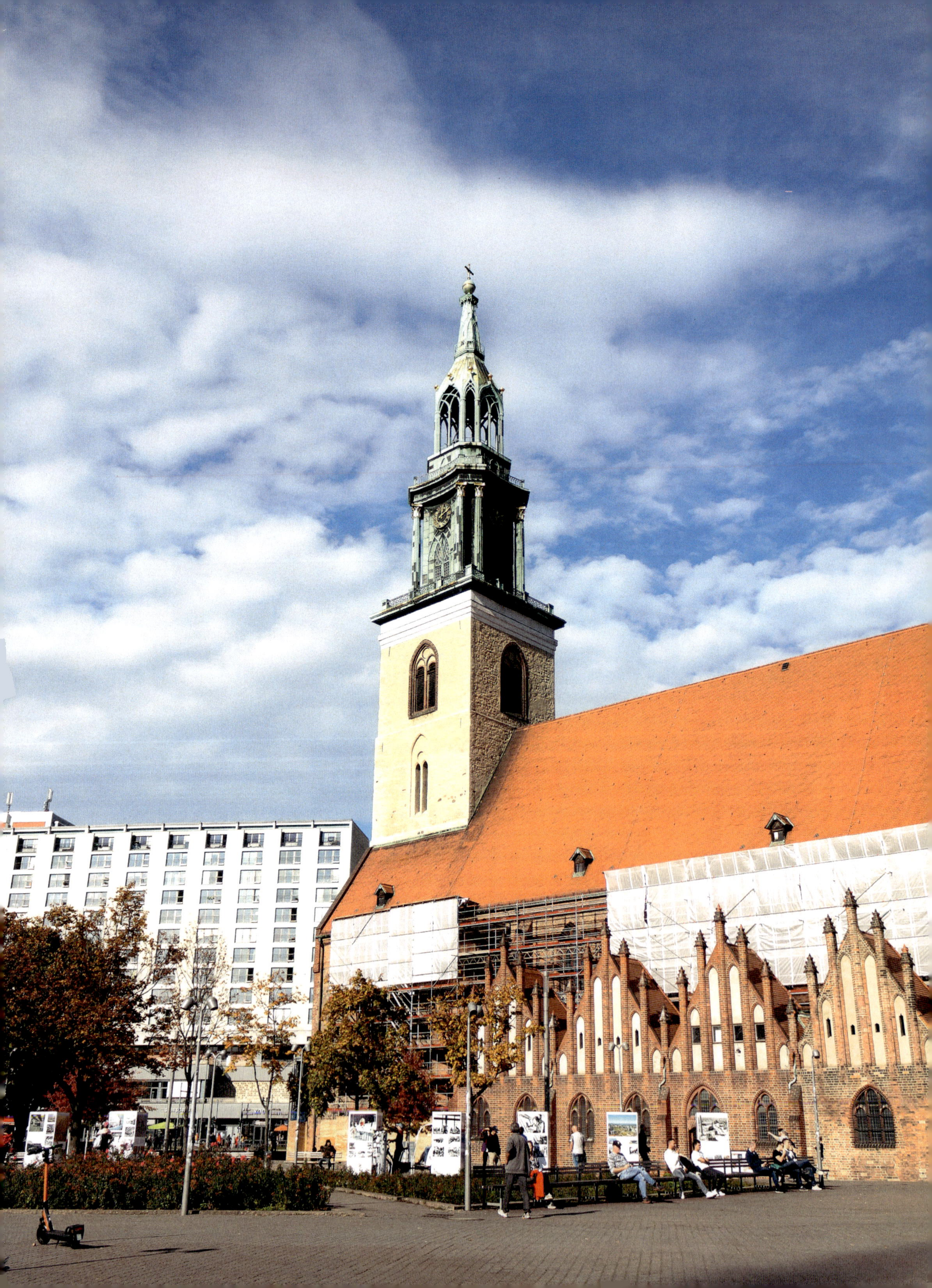

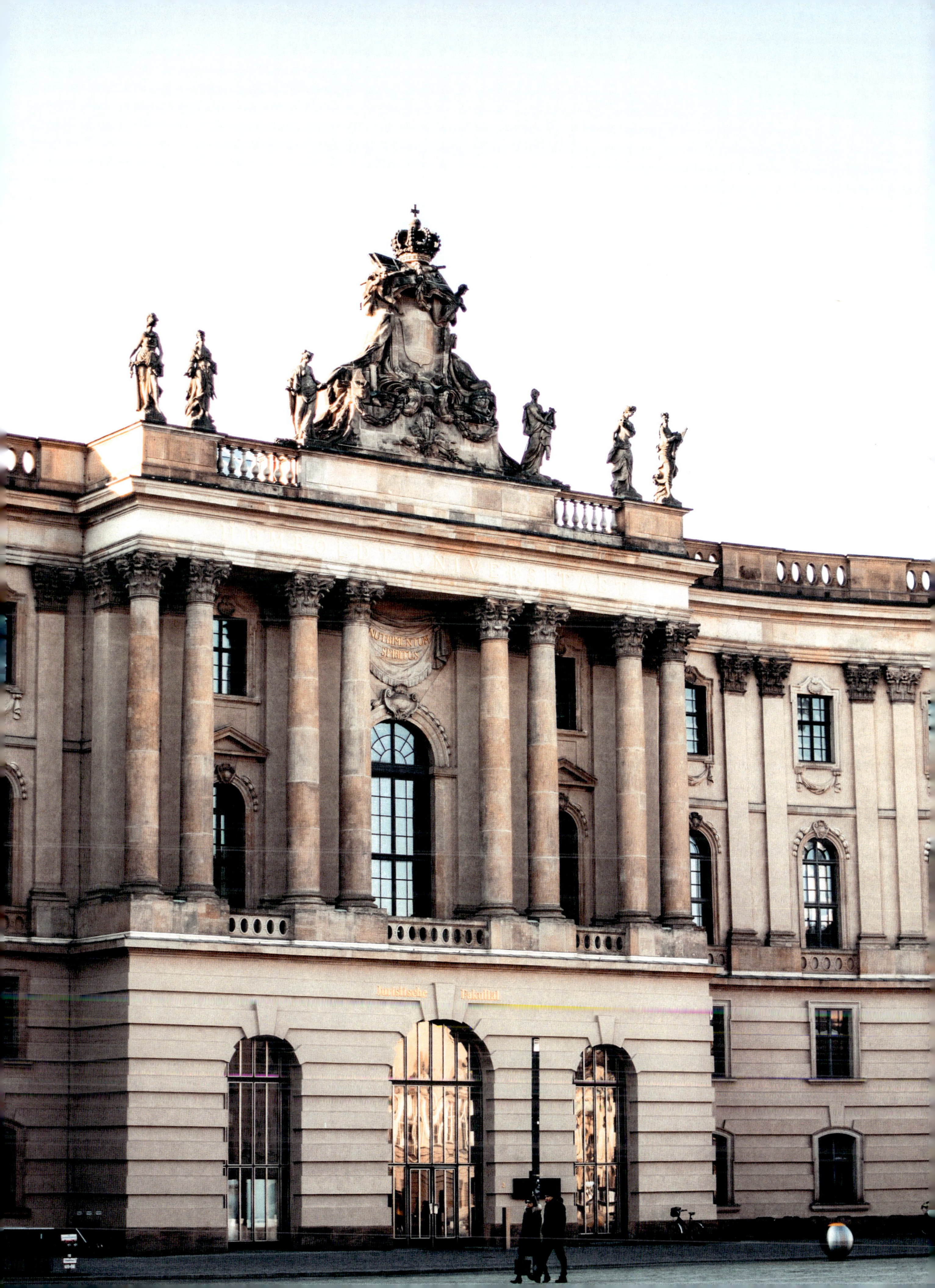
NUTRIMENTUM

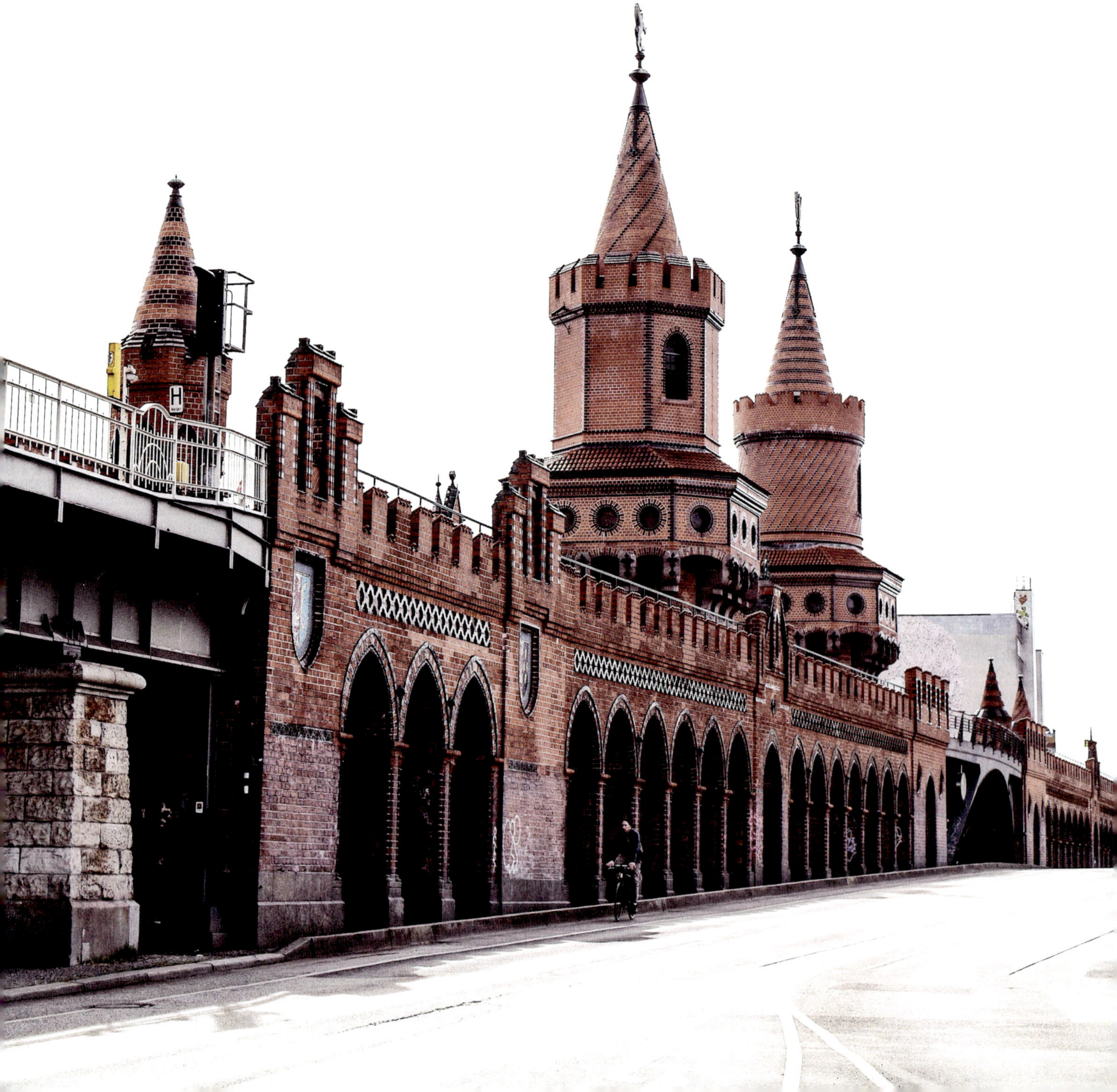
H

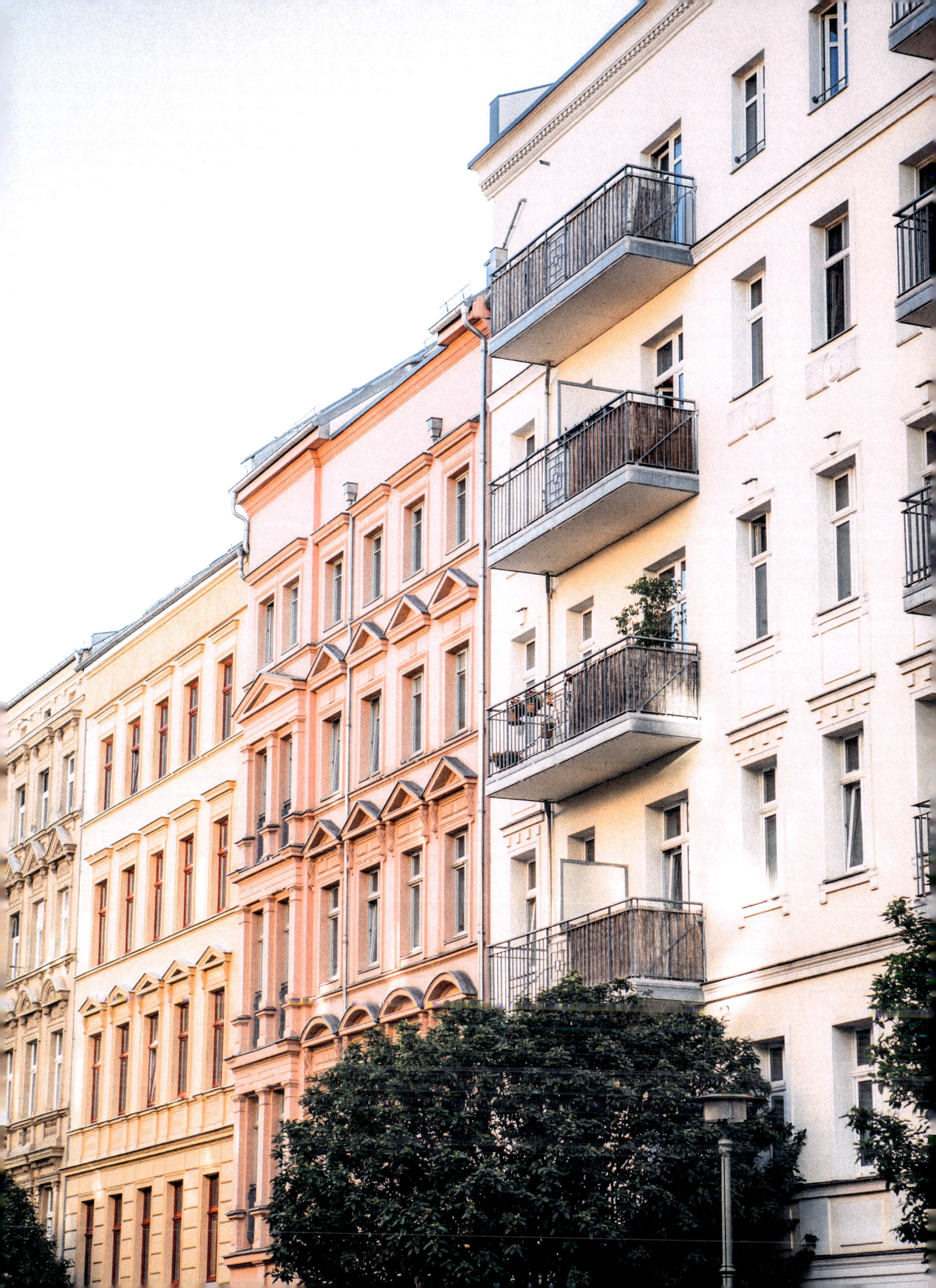

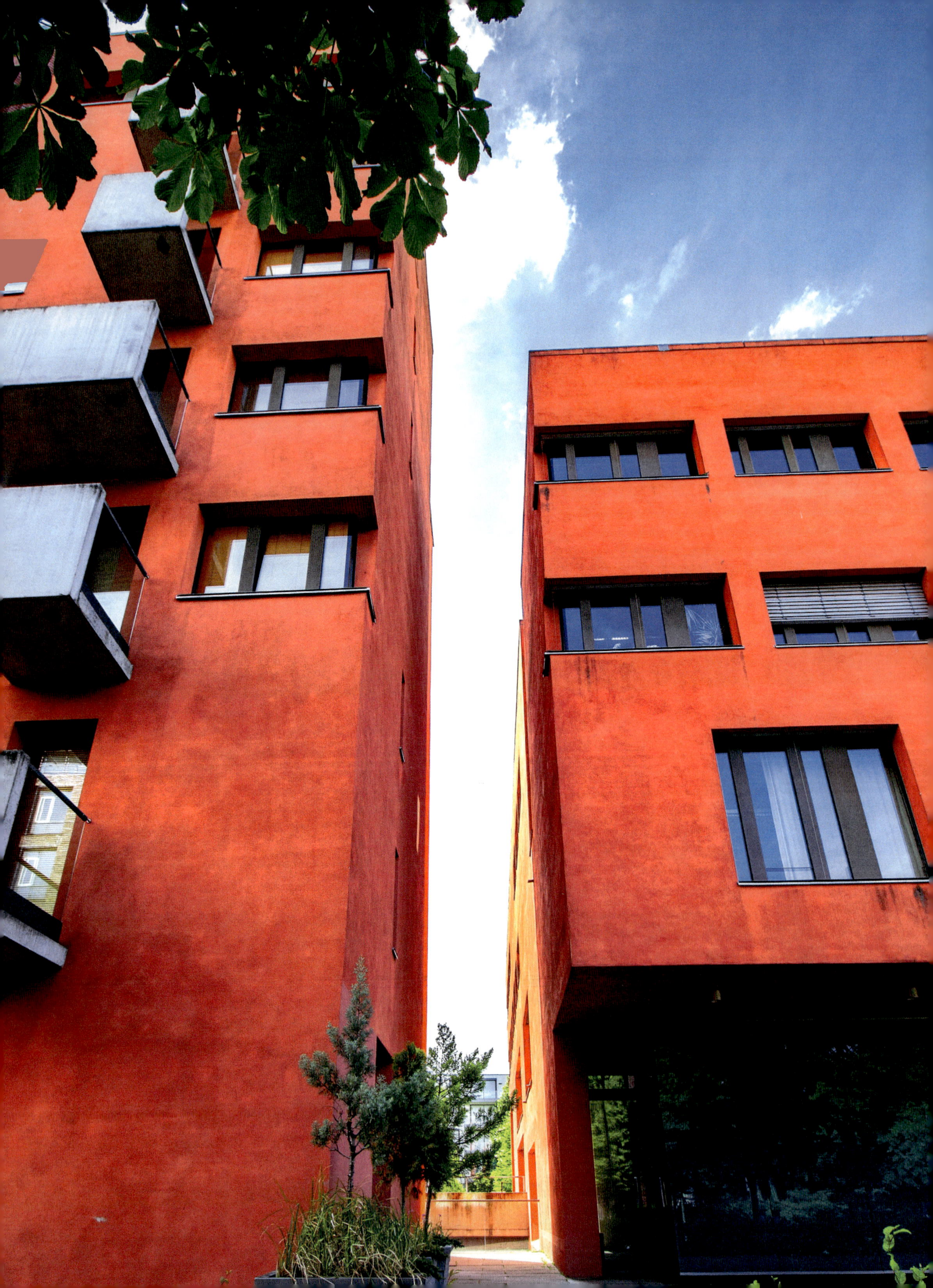

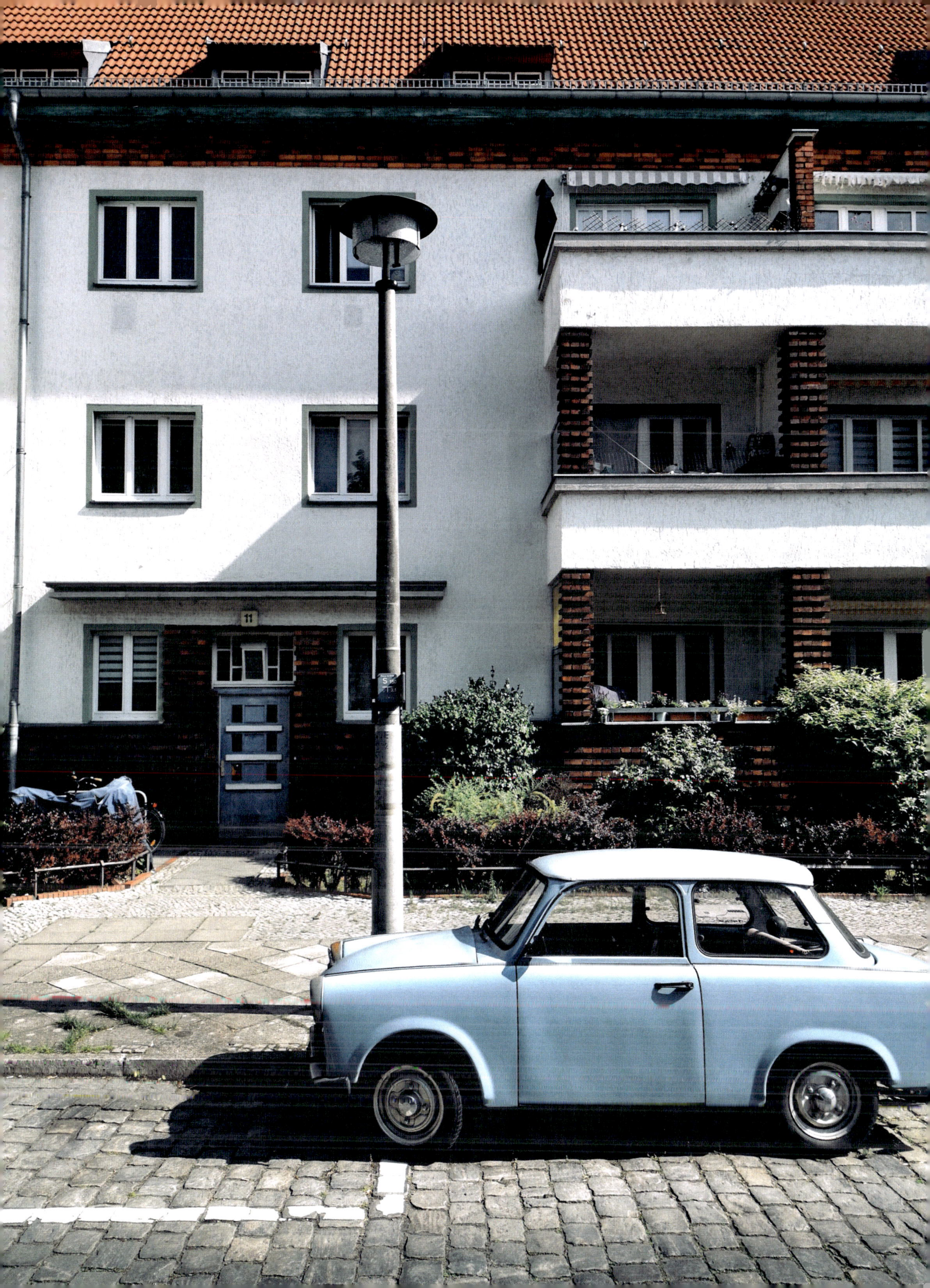
11

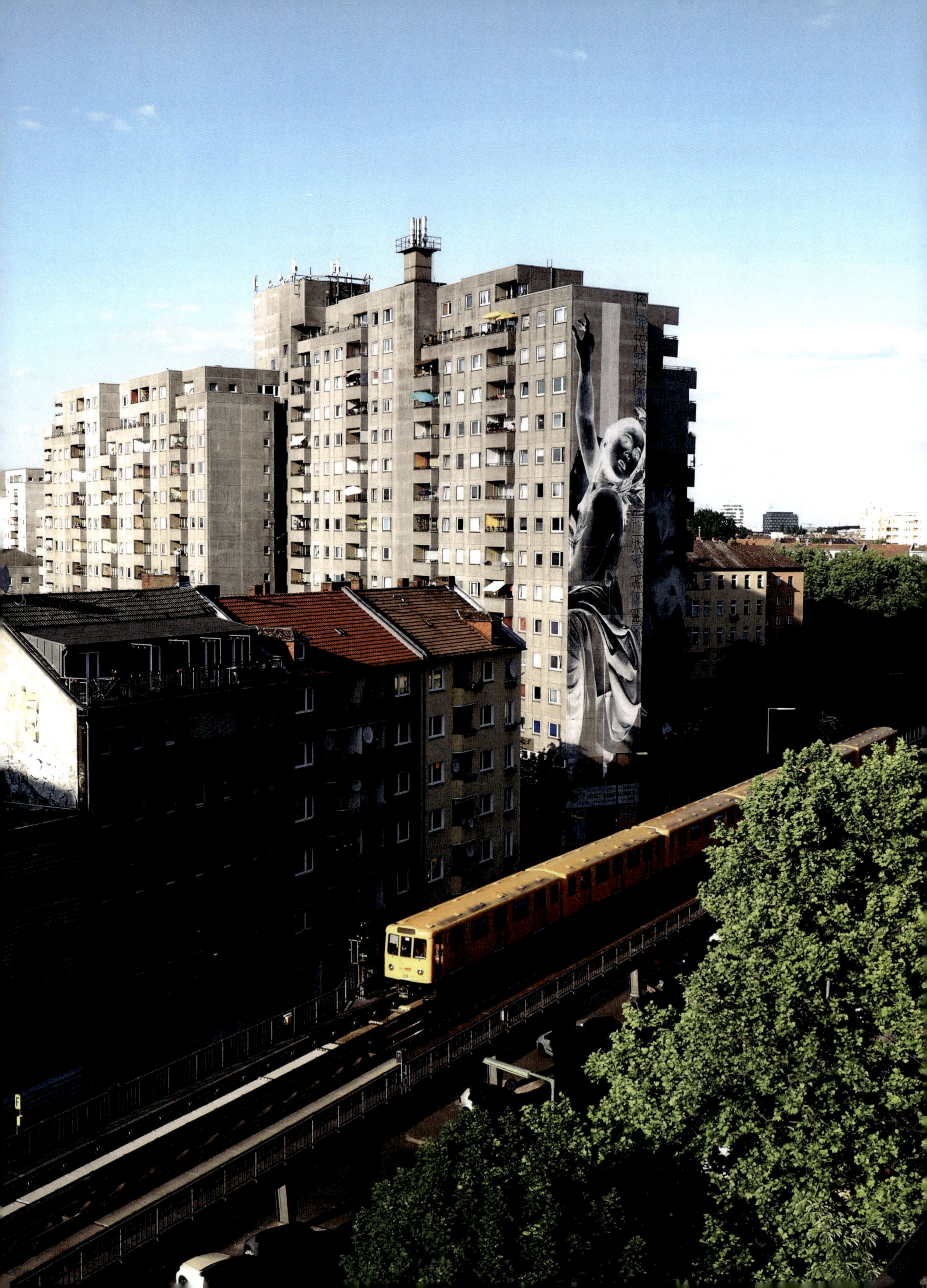

St. Hedwig-
Krankenhaus
Große Hamburger Straße
Krausnickstraße
zu vermieten
0178 330 12 68
stich immobilien

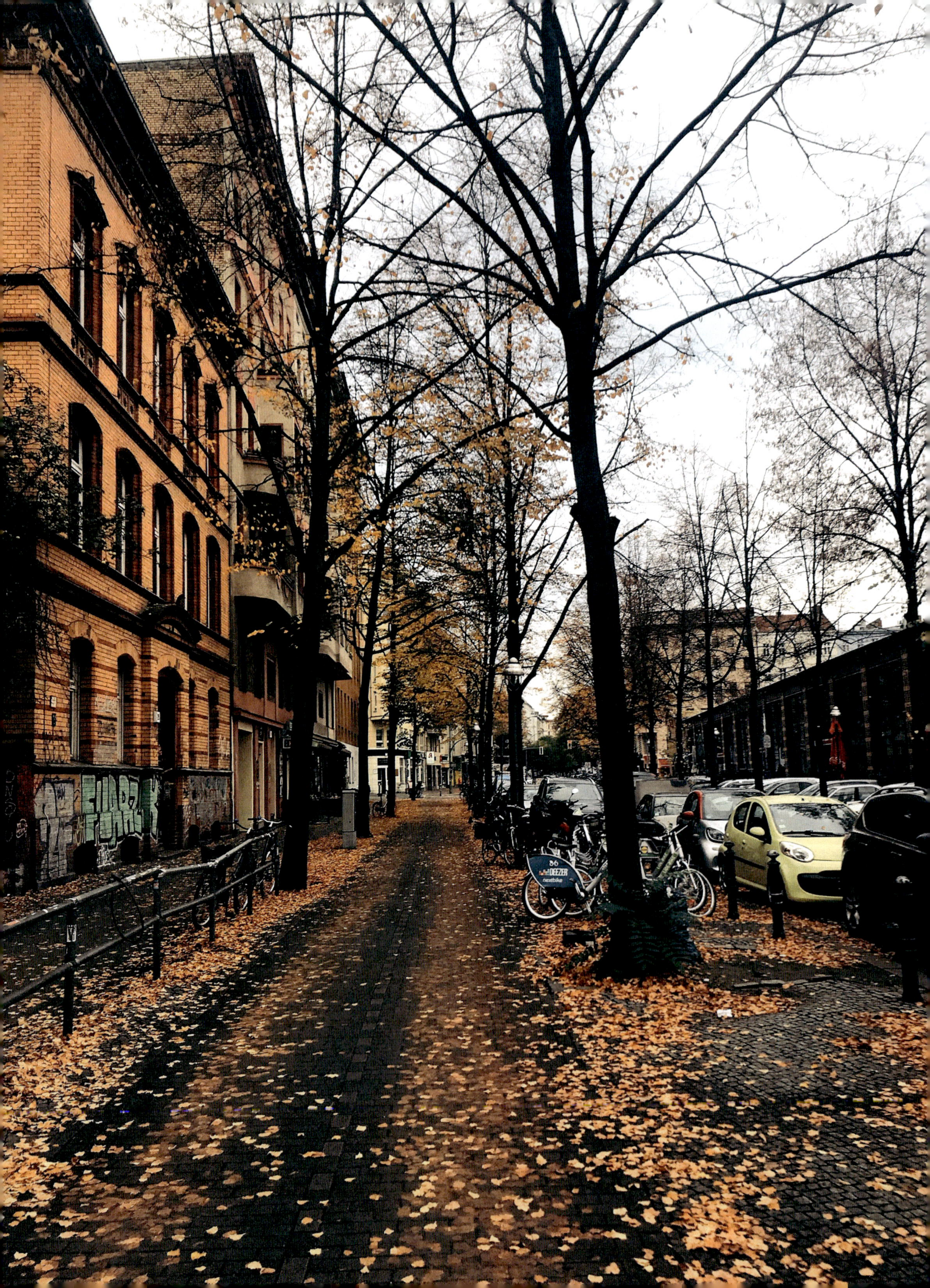

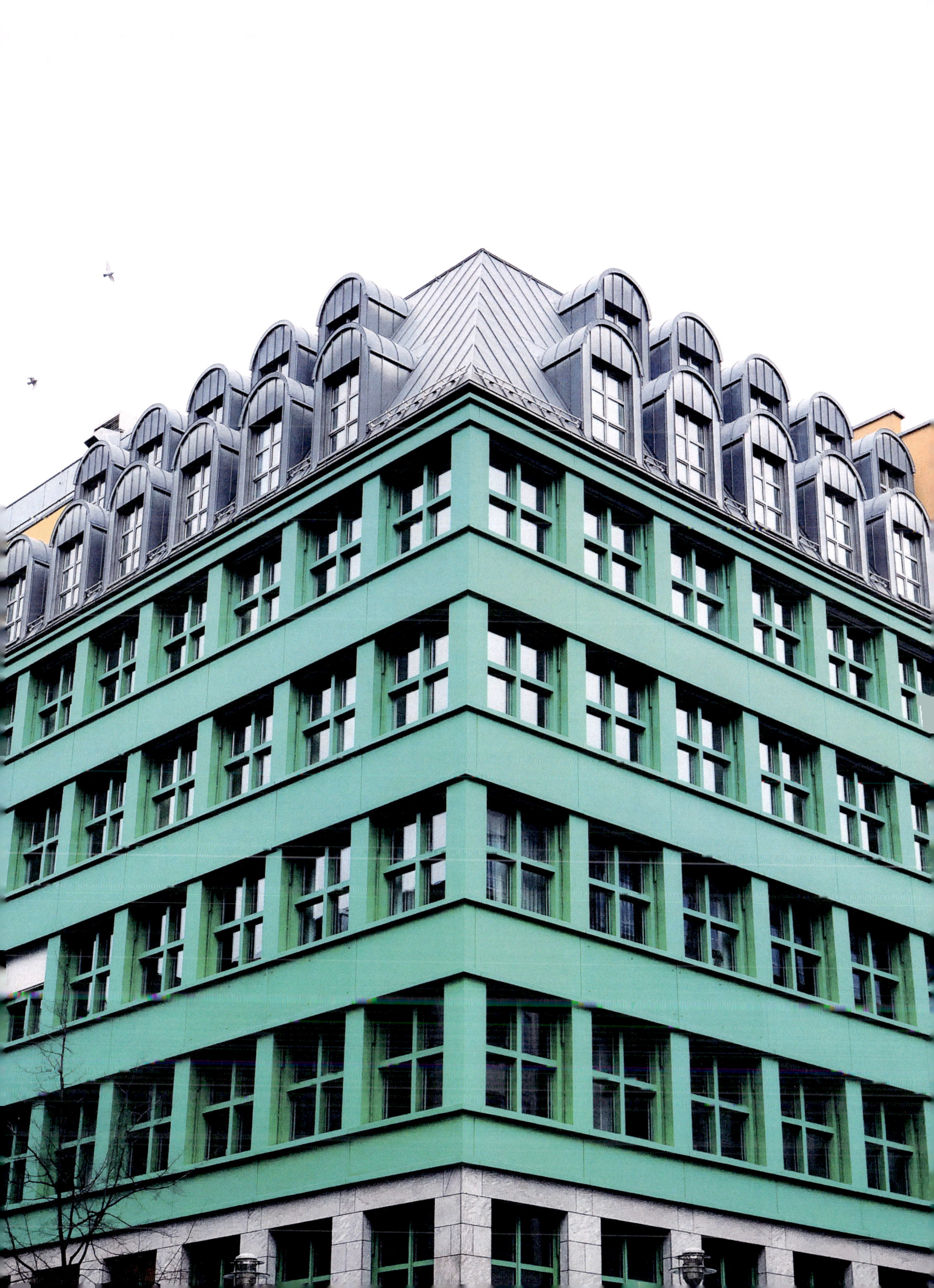

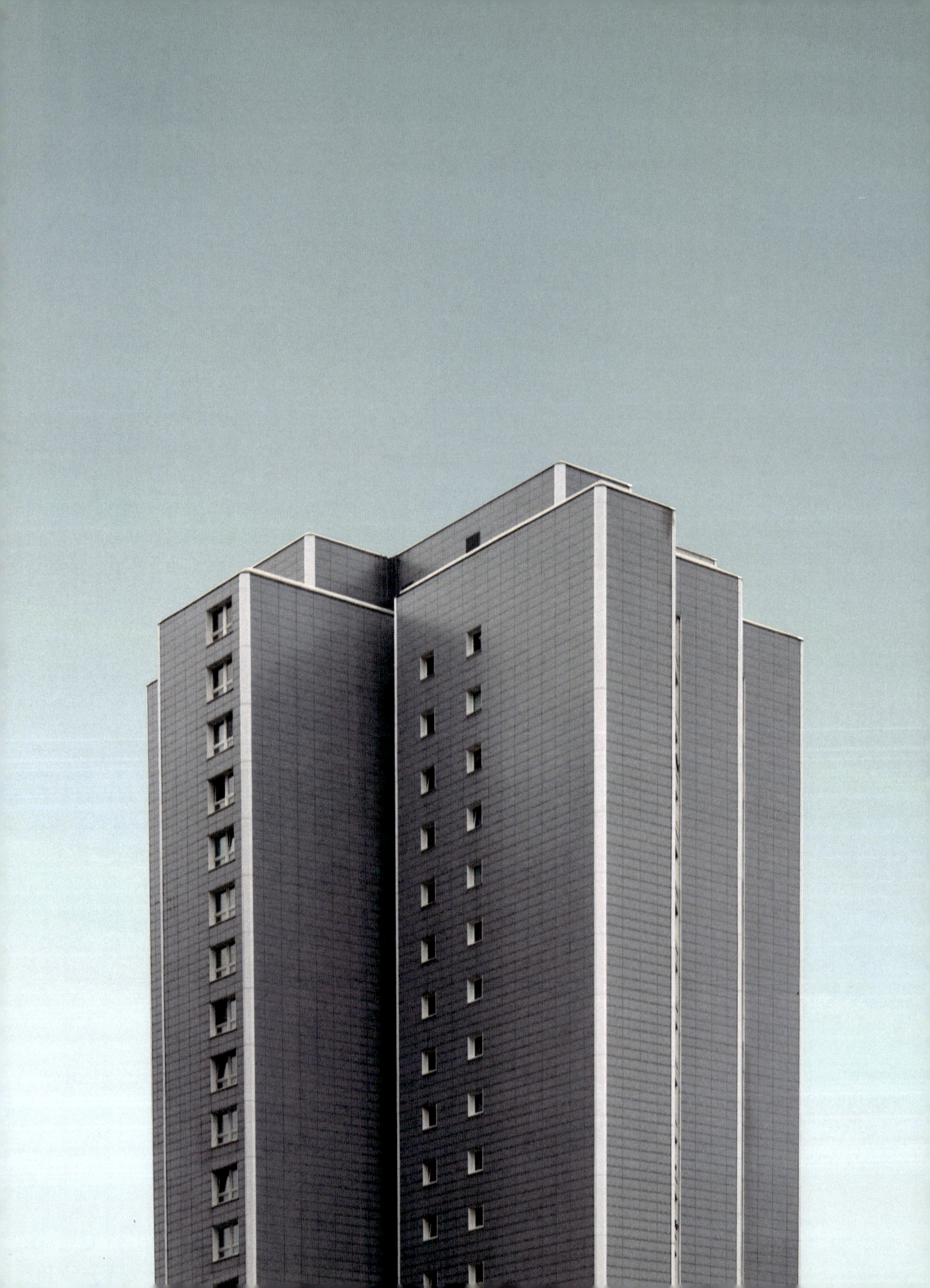

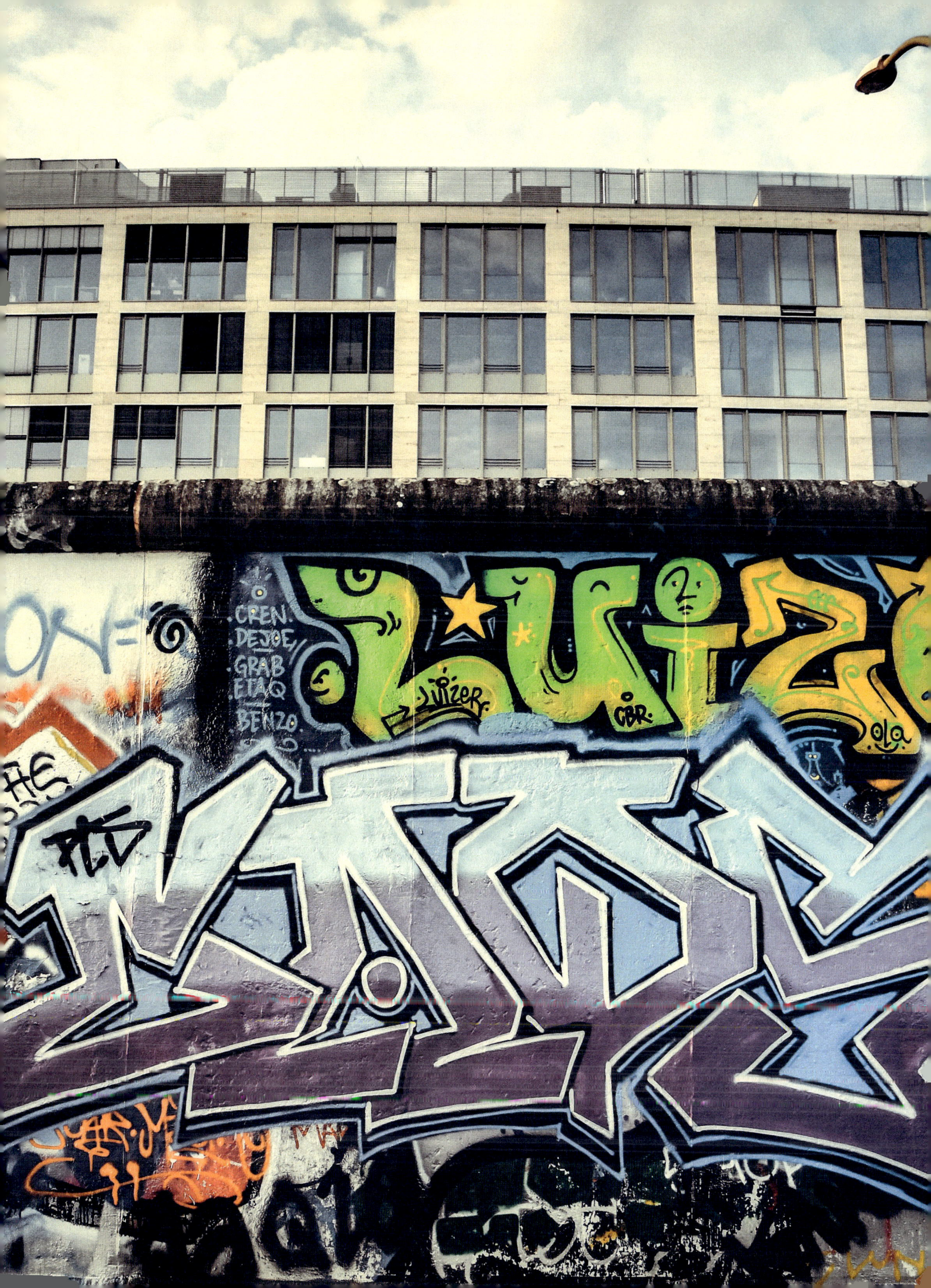
CREN.
DEJOE
GRAB
ETAQ
BENZO
LUIZER
CBR.
OLA

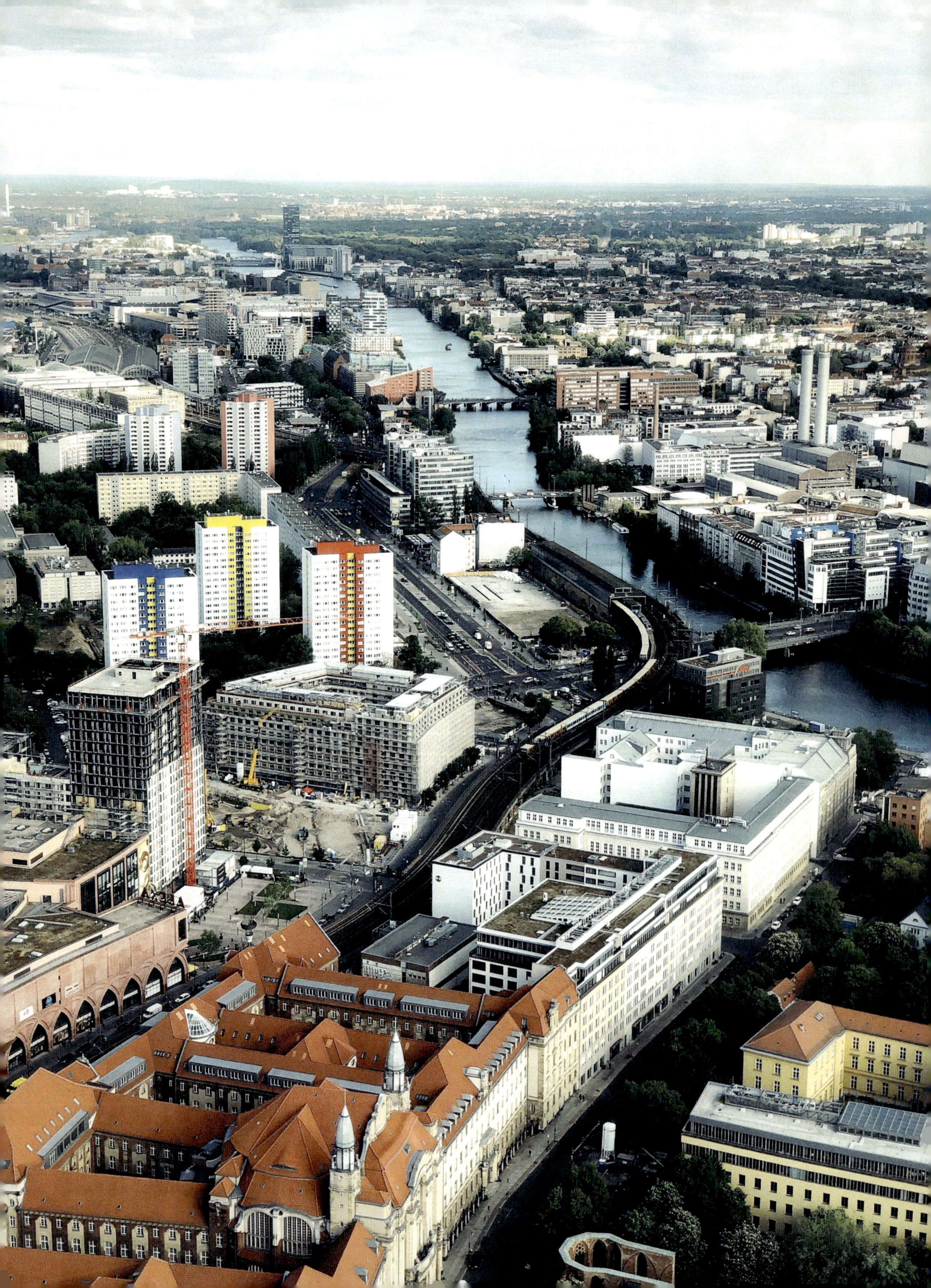

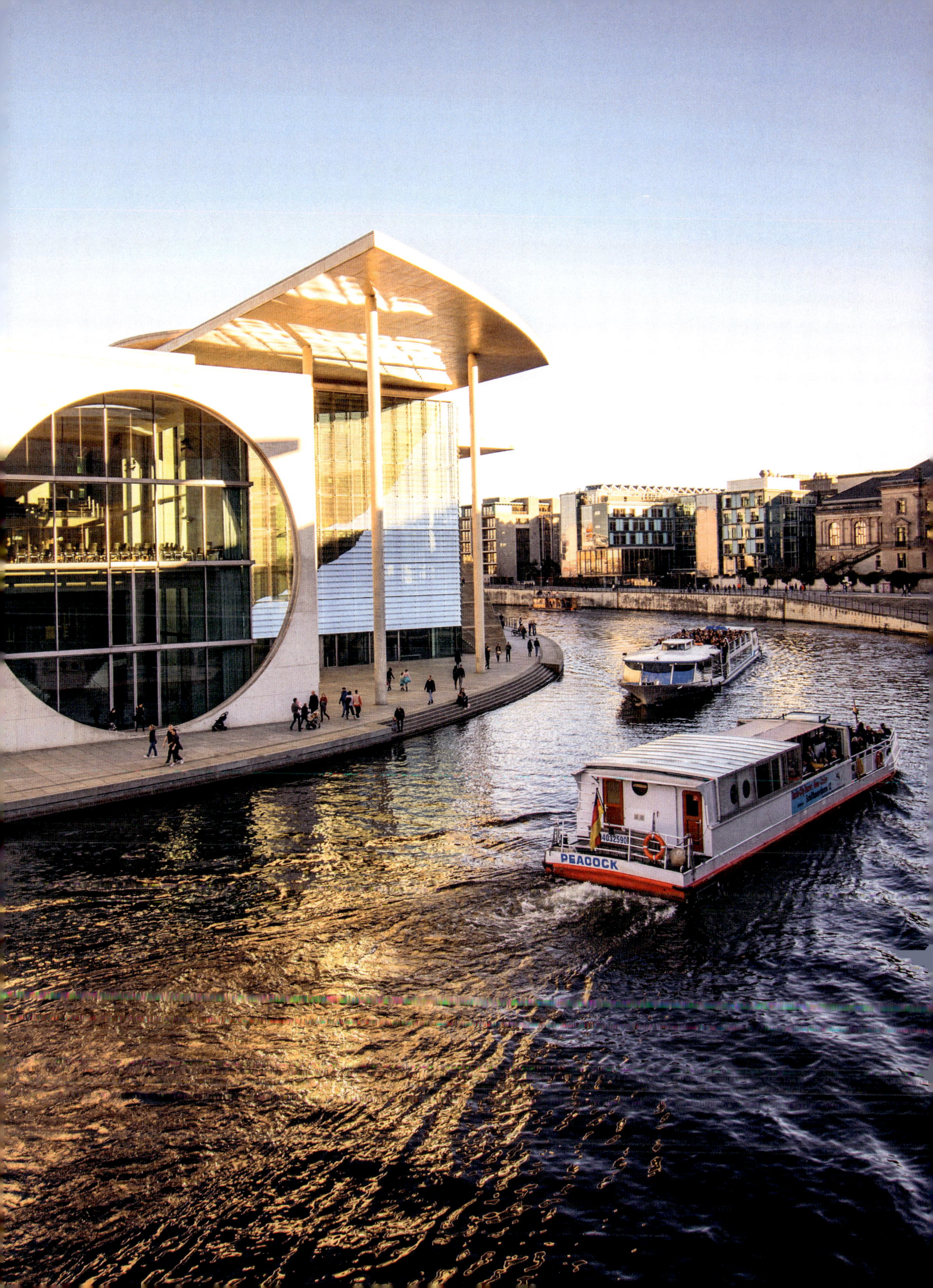
4032590
PEACOCK

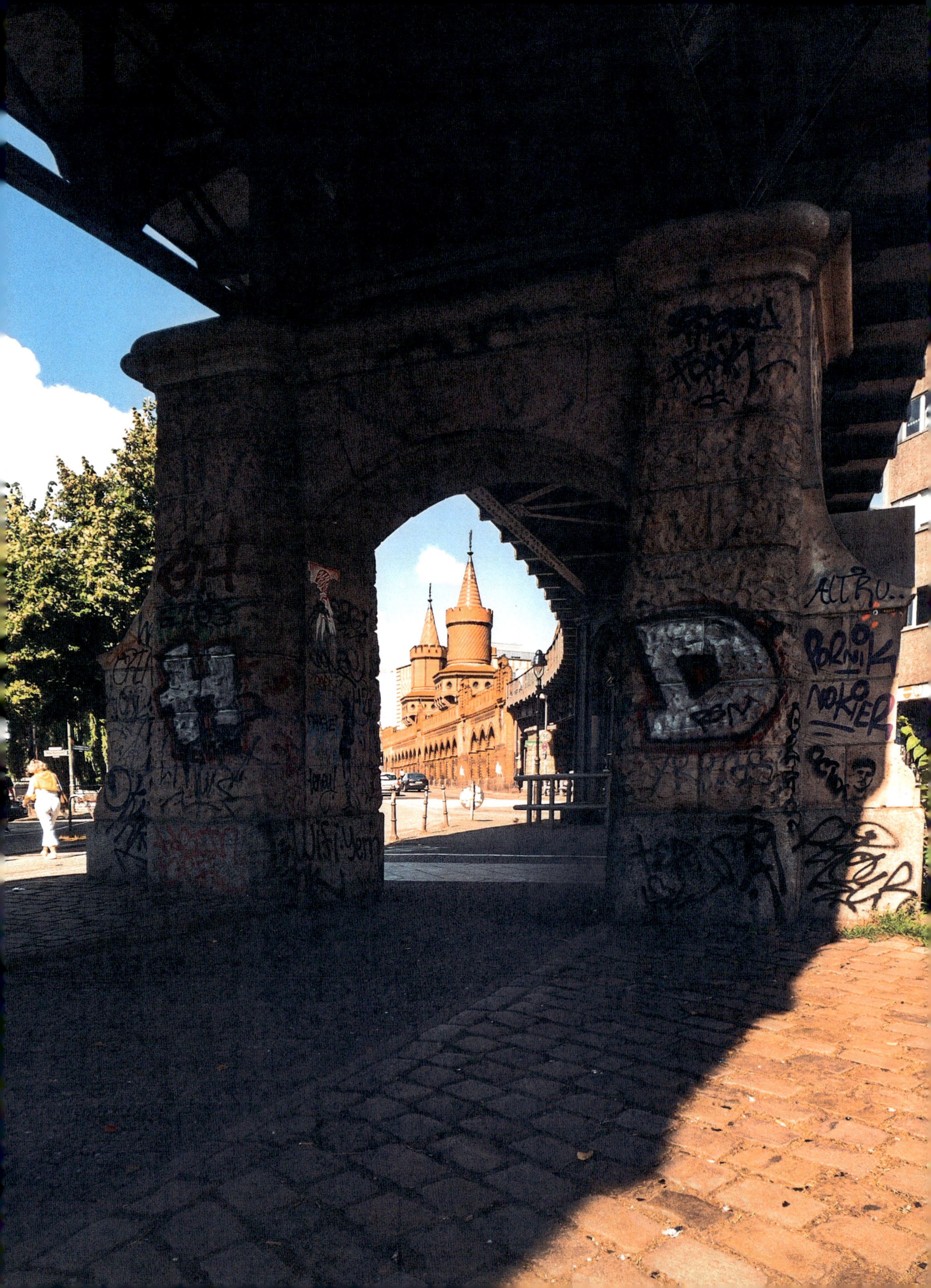

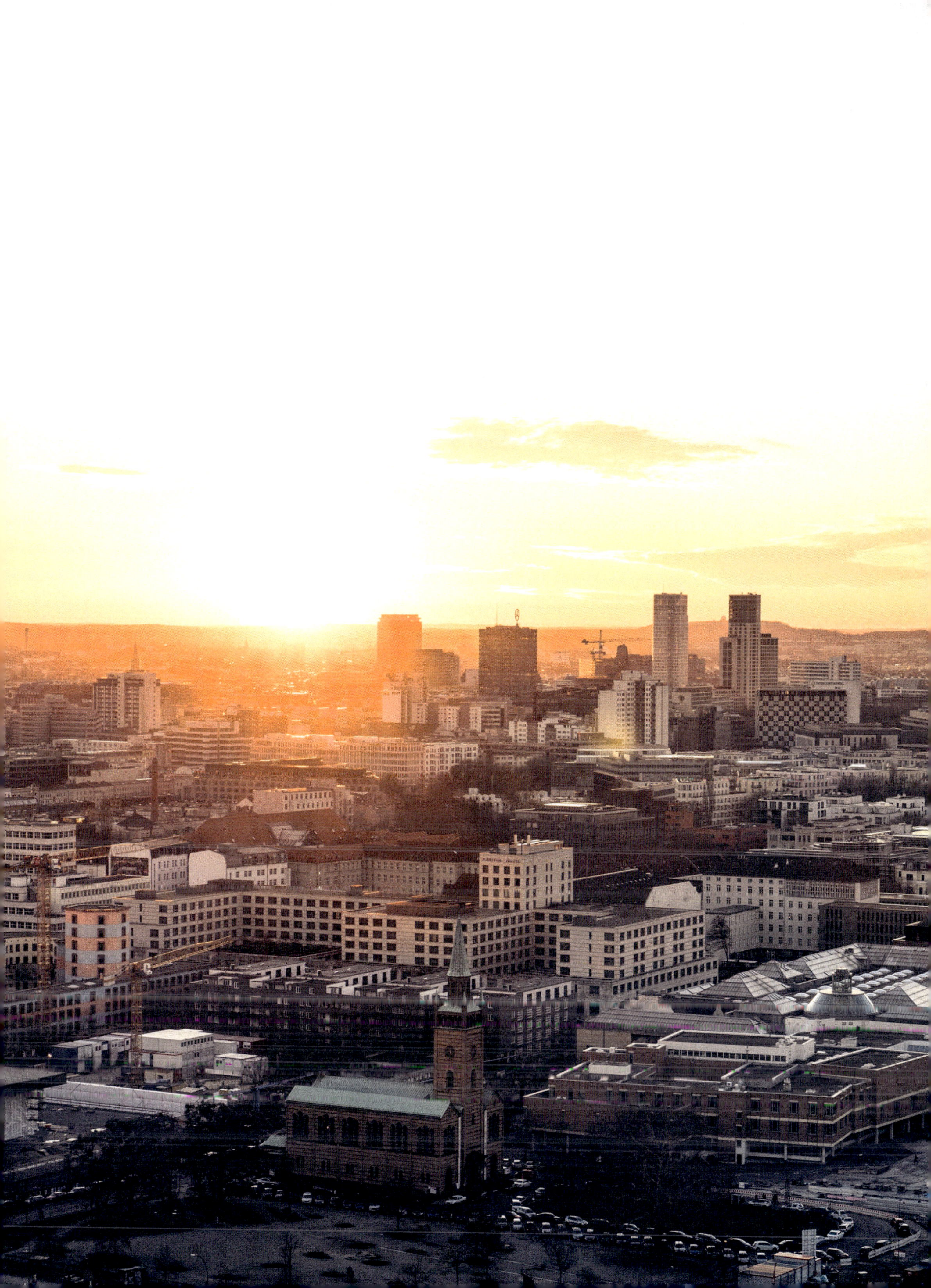

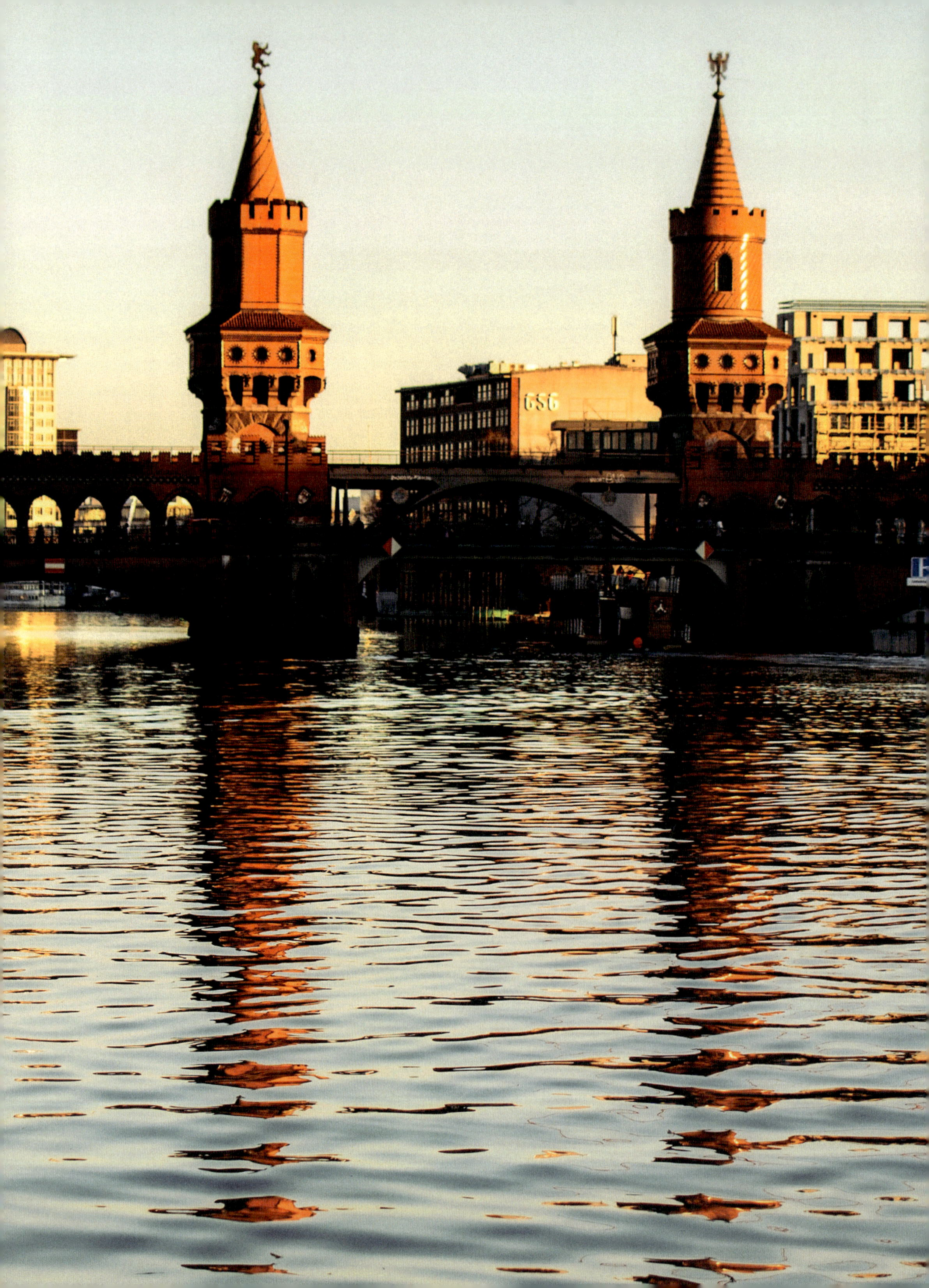

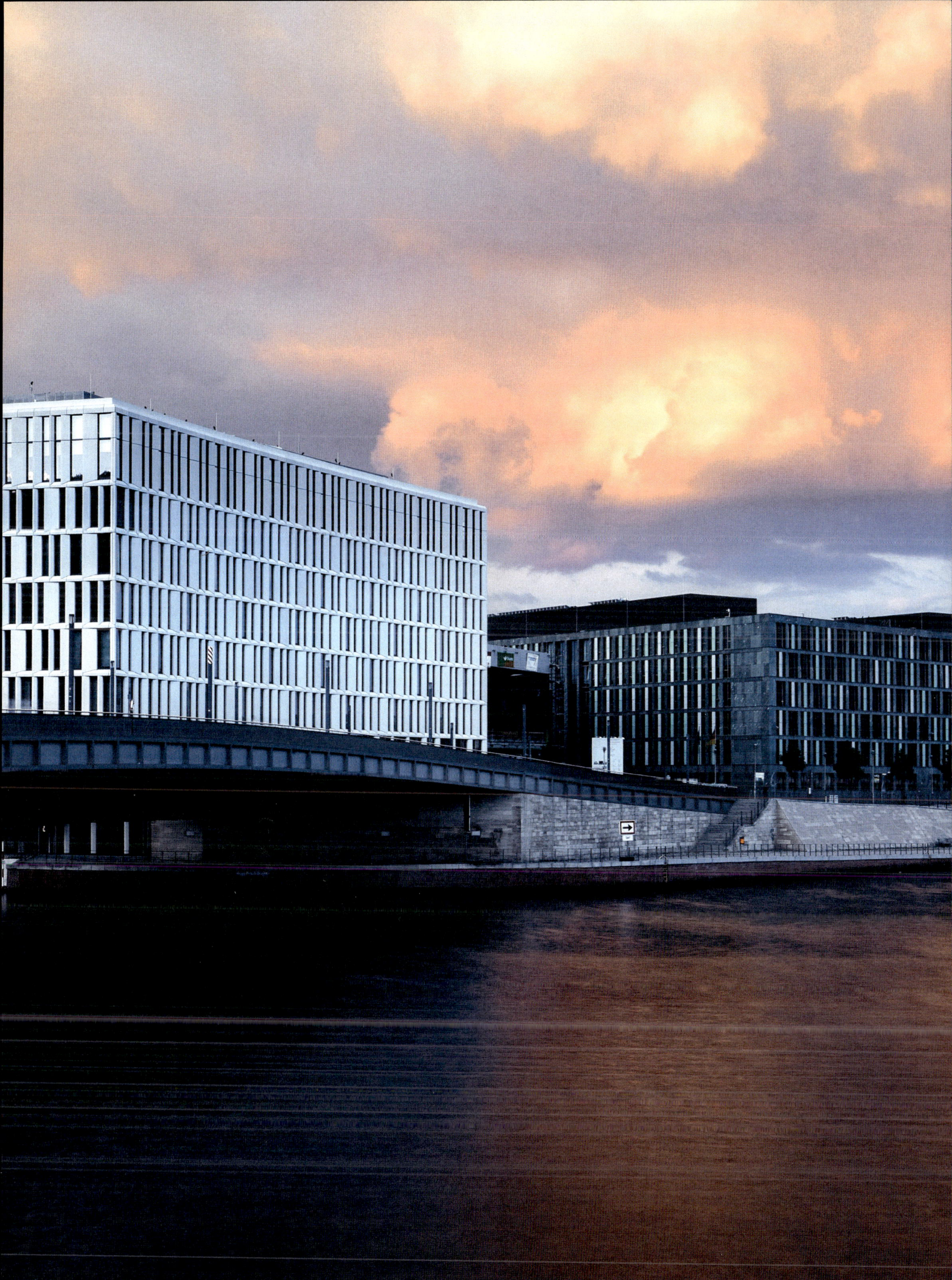

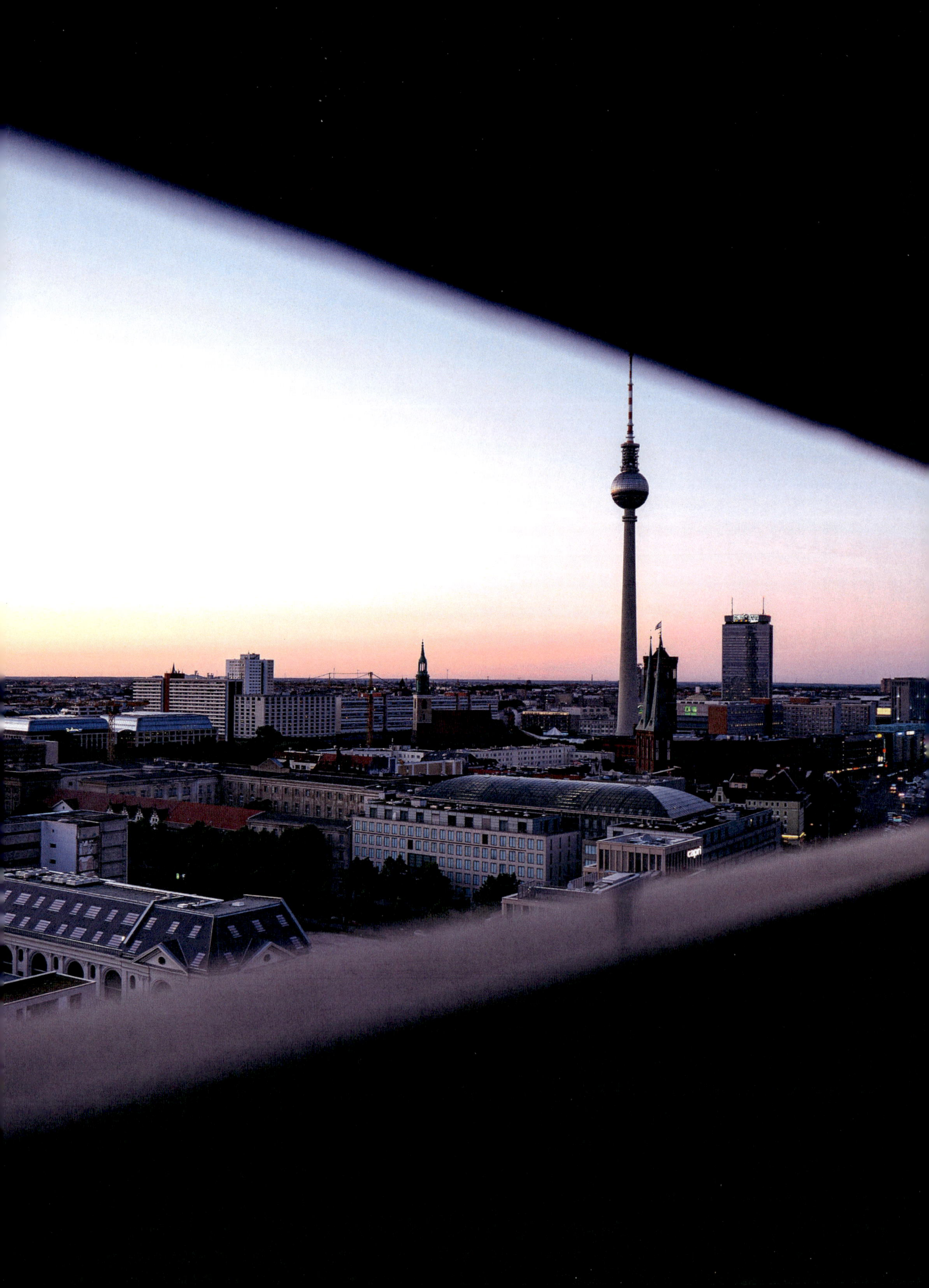
capri

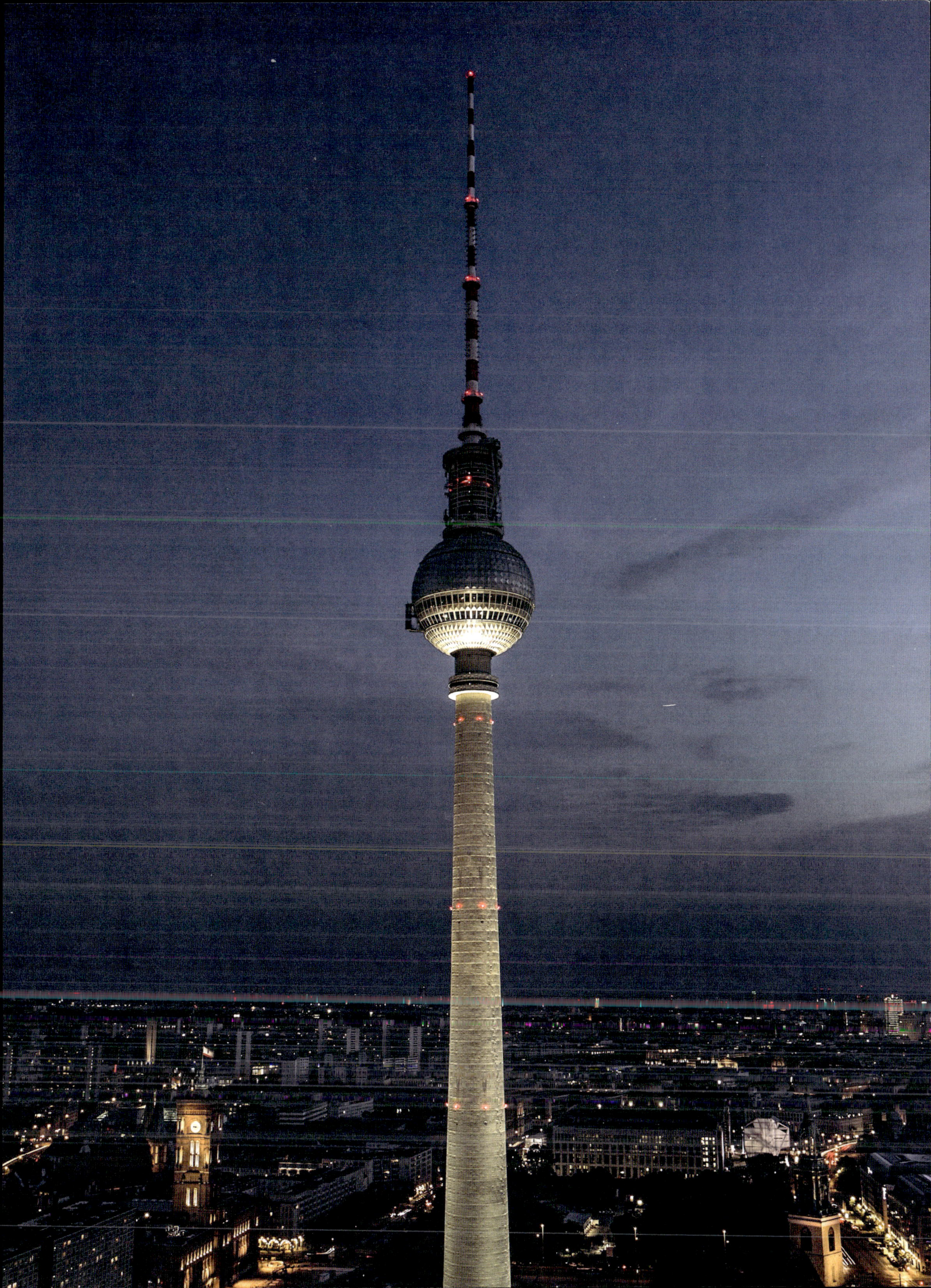

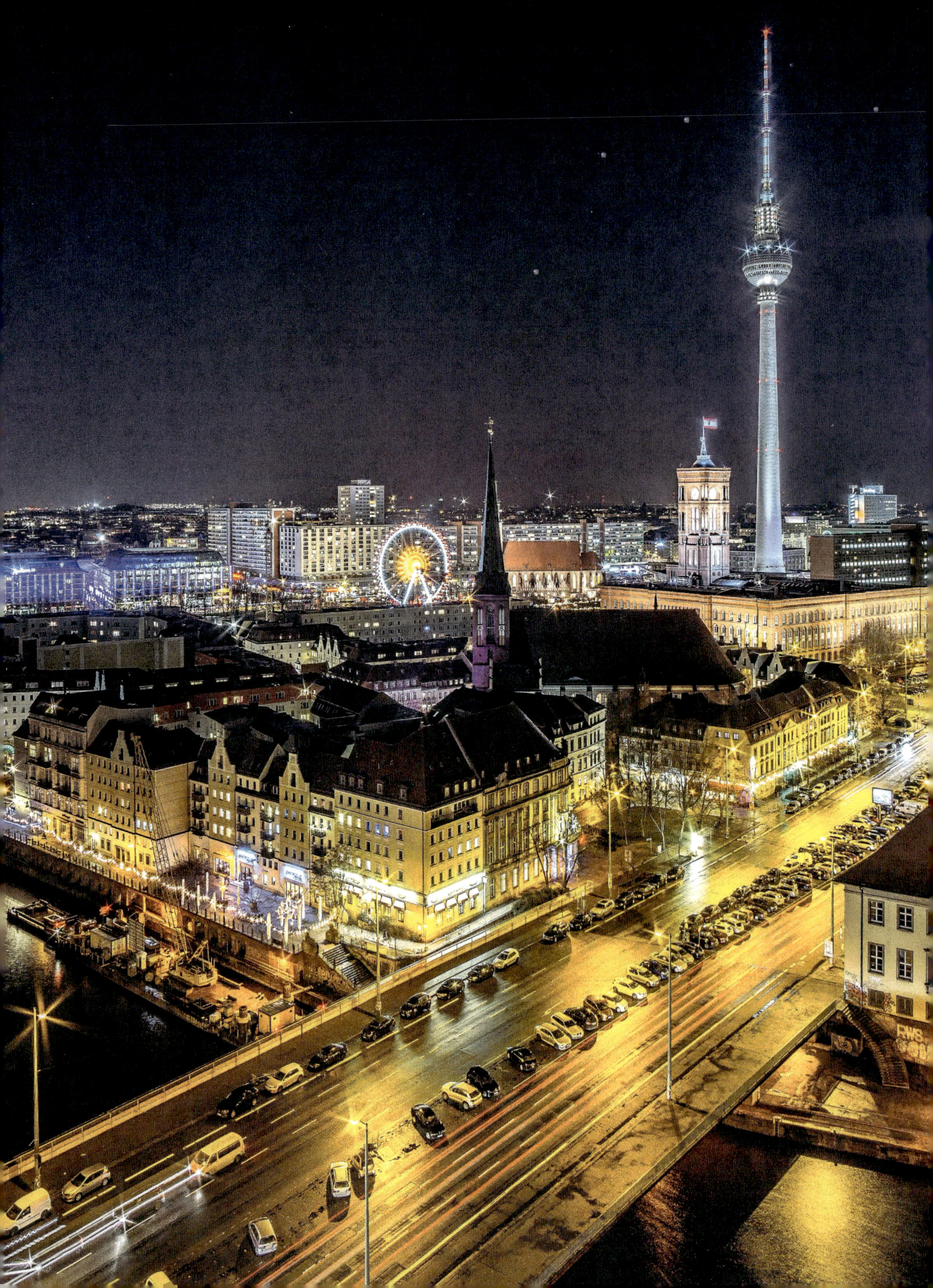

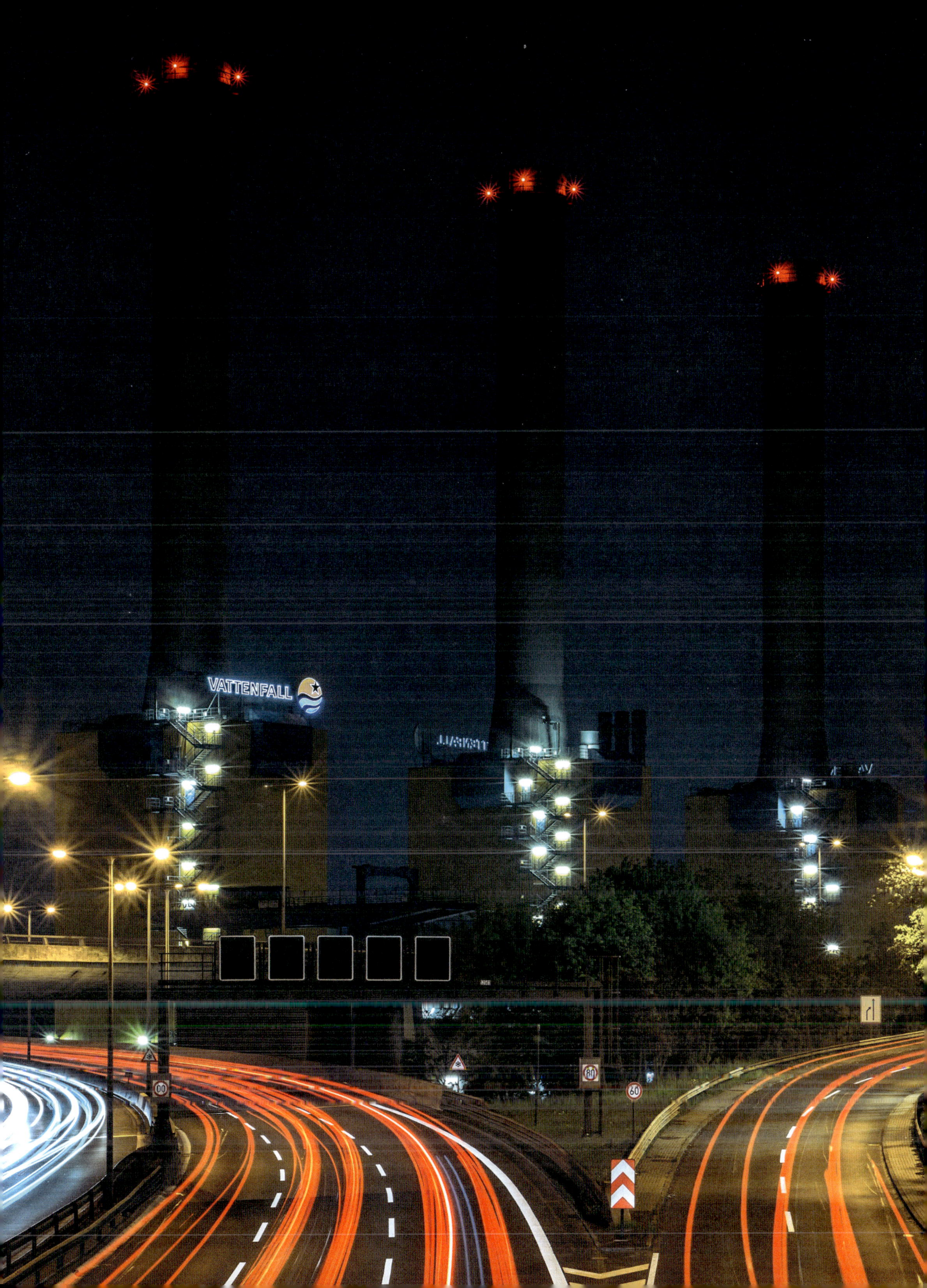
VATTENFALL
60

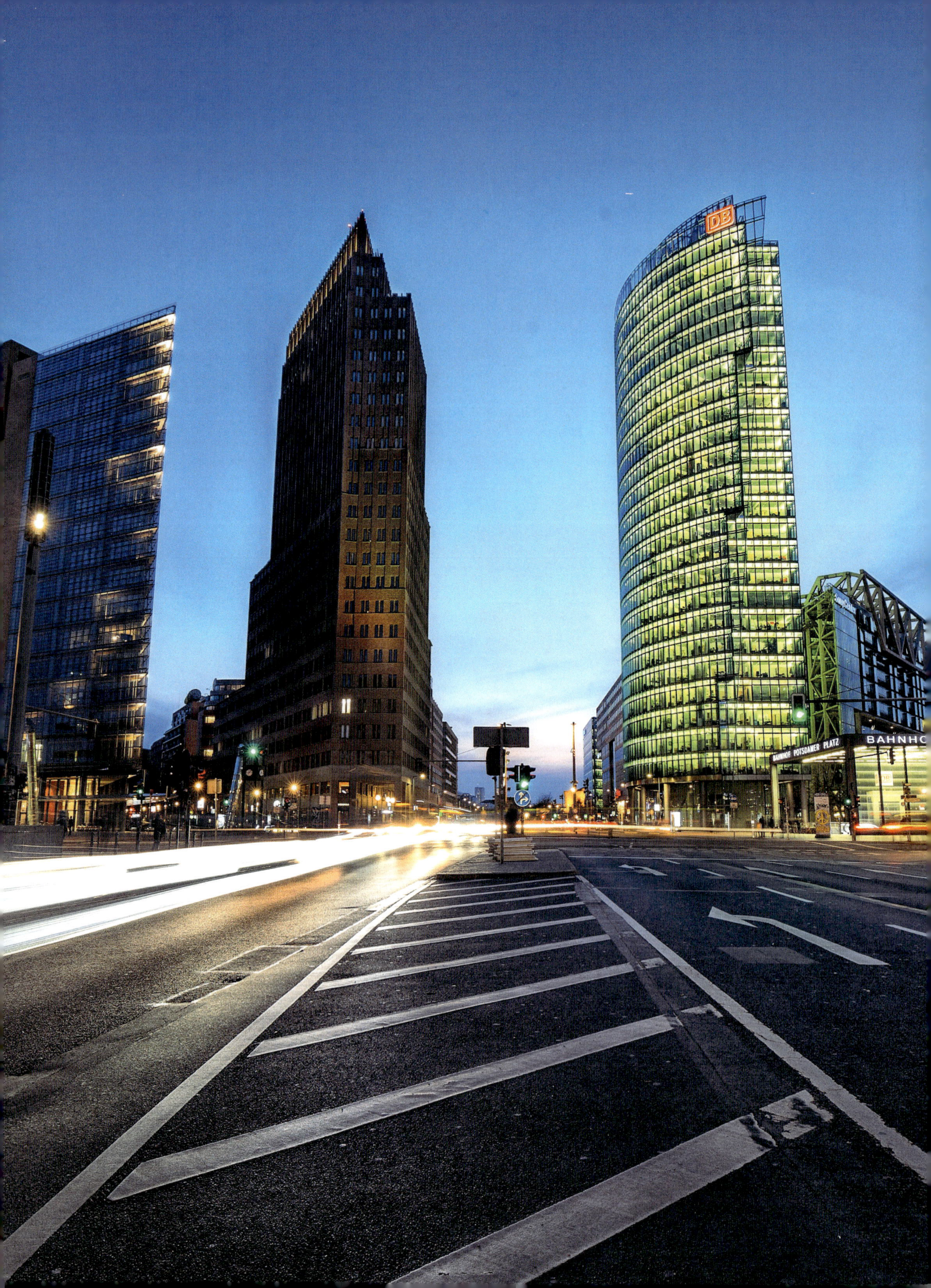
DB
BAHNHOF POTSDAMER PLATZ
BAHNHO

Made in the USA
Coppell, TX
17 June 2021